JUNIOR GREAT BOOKS

SUN SERIES
VOLUME 3

The Great Books Foundation

A nonprofit educational corporation

20 19

Printed in the United States of America

Published and distributed by

THE GREAT BOOKS FOUNDATION

A nonprofit educational corporation

35 East Wacker Drive, Suite 400

Chicago, IL 60601

Note to the At-Home Reader

Read the assigned story aloud, making sure your child can see the text and pictures as you read. Ask your child to say the underlined phrases in the book with you. Whenever the character "G.B." (pictured above) appears, you will know that you should ask your child the question in the box. Give your child time to think through and talk over his or her answer. Whenever you can, ask your child **why** he or she gave that answer. Keep in mind that these are open-ended questions for which there are no single right answers. When G.B.'s question calls for an answer to be marked, help your child do so.

When you have finished the reading, ask your child what question he or she has about the story. Write this question on the lines provided at the end of the selection.

For the "Mysterious Animals" poetry unit, read "The Song of the Jellicles" once through, asking your child to chorus the underlined phrases with you. Then read the poem a second time, discussing G.B.'s questions as they occur.

Your child will read and discuss the other two poems, "If You Go Softly" and "The Six Badgers," later, in class, but feel free to enjoy these poems together at any time.

The blank pages in this book are for activities that will be completed in class. Encourage your child to show you his or her work when each unit is finished.

THE KING OF THE FROGS

AFRICAN FOLKTALE

The Frogs Do As They Please

Have you ever been beside a lake in Africa at night and listened to the frogs? You haven't? Then you cannot imagine what the noise is like. And it's not just one kind of noise, it's several. Over there for instance are a thousand creaking doors that have never had their hinges oiled and someone opens and shuts them—and keeps on doing just that. Over *there* are a thousand fat men snoring and no one wakes them up. Then there are a thousand carpenters sawing planks and all the saws want a touch of grease, and a thousand little bells are being struck and a thousand corks are being pulled out of bottles.

Noise! You can hardly hear yourself think.

Then you go a little closer until you can just see the edge of the water and perhaps a reed or two and there is silence. Just the splash of a frog jumping into the water late because he was asleep and didn't hear you coming. Then nothing, and you can hear the whole world breathe.

There's a story about this.

Long ago the frogs did as they pleased and the result was dreadful. Not one of them would listen to what another said and they all shouted at once. Children wouldn't obey their parents and even wives wouldn't listen to their husbands, which is, indeed, something hardly to be understood. It was all noisy and untidy beyond bearing and nothing ever got done.

At last a wise, wise old frog called everyone to a meeting and, since he had a very fine voice and went on shouting for long enough, he managed to get them all there at once, for to tell you the truth they were pretty sick of living the way they did.

"Frogs!" said the old frog, puffing himself up. "We cannot go on like this. It's no sort of life for anyone and, anyway, when you see how all the other creatures live it makes one ashamed of being a frog. There is only one thing to do. We must get a king. When people have kings there is peace and order and everyone does as he is told."

"Agreed!" they all shouted and they stayed long enough to commission the old frog to see what he could do about getting them one, before everybody fell to quarreling and pushing and splashing and the meeting broke up in disorder. As usual.

Then the wise, wise old frog went to see the Great God **Mmumi** (you will say the two *m*'s correctly if you hum a little before you begin the word). Mmumi happened to be in charge of that part of the world.

Mmumi

He is a very slow god and usually gives people more than they bargain for. He agreed drowsily that the frogs needed a king and promised to do something about it. Then he went to sleep again.

So the frogs went on as usual, which was badly, until one day Mmumi woke up, remembered his promise, took a great green mossy boulder which had the rough shape of a gigantic frog and threw it into the water. **SPLASH!**

"There you are!" he shouted (it sounded like thunder). "There's your king. His name's Gogo and like me he doesn't want to be disturbed. Respect him and be satisfied."

12

Do you think Mmumi gives the frogs Gogo because Mmumi is:

LAZY

WISE

MAKING FUN OF THEM

(Circle your answer.)

The whole lake was shaken by
Gogo's fall. The waves washed through
the reeds and tore up the shore,
and in the middle of a great cloud of
mud Gogo settled on the bottom and
the fat green waterweeds curled round
and over him. He looked shocking.

The frogs were terrified and fled
under stones and into dark corners
and holes under the bank. Their long
white legs streaked behind them as they
swam. Parents found their children
and husbands their wives and then
settled down to explaining what
had happened.

"This is our king," they said, "and a fine terrible one he seems, and from the splash he made not the sort to fool about with. Now all will be well and this scandalous behavior will stop."

And so it did, for a while.

But although Gogo had made such a wonderful first impression, as time passed they noticed that he never moved. He just sat quietly in the mud and stared in the same direction. Presently they began to get used to him, until finally some young, bold, bad frogs ventured to swim close to him and then one of them touched his nose.

And still Gogo said and did nothing.

"Bah! He's not a king!" they shouted. **"He's not even a frog.** He's just an old stone and couldn't hurt anyone." And they swam round him until they were dizzy and jumped all over his back and went away and spoke rudely about him to their elders.

Do you agree that the young frogs are "bad"? (Circle your answer.)

YES   NO

Why or why not?

14

At first none of the elders believed them. They had told their children Gogo was a king and a king he had to be, but soon it was impossible to deny that the children were right and then . . . . Well, the noise began again and things were as they had always been, only worse. **Terrible!**

The wise, wise old frog sighed and set out to see Mmumi again, who was not at all pleased at being woken a second time.

"All right!" he shouted in a passion. "*All right!* You aren't satisfied with the king I've given you. Is that the way it is? Very well, you shall have another and I hope you like him."

And the very next night he gave them Mamba the Crocodile.

Gogo had come to his people with a splash that shook the lake

but Mamba slid into the water with only
a whisper and left but one small
ring spreading gently to show that he
had come. Then he swam, silent
as a shadow, lithe and long and secret,
his jaws grinning like a trap. Gogo
had never visited the people he had been
given to rule but Mamba visited them
often and suddenly, and whenever he met
a subject the great jaws gaped and closed
and often it was the last of that frog.

The frogs developed the greatest
respect for their new king and lived
quietly, looking over the backs of their
heads as frogs can. Now and again at
night they break out but they keep their
ears open and if you go near the lake
they shut up.

They think that it's Mamba coming to
put a little order into them and they
keep quiet.

Does Mmumi give
the frogs Mamba for
a king to punish
them or to make
their life better?
(Circle your answer.)

TO PUNISH THEM

TO MAKE THEIR
LIFE BETTER

King Mamba and His Subjects

What do *you* think the frogs should do? (Circle one.)

1. Have a frog king

2. Have another animal as king

3. Make their own rules

Why? _____

_____

_____

_____

Quiet and Noisy

In a quiet mood, I _____

_____

_____

_____

_____

In a noisy mood, I _____

_____

_____

_____

My Question

_____

_____

_____

Name _____

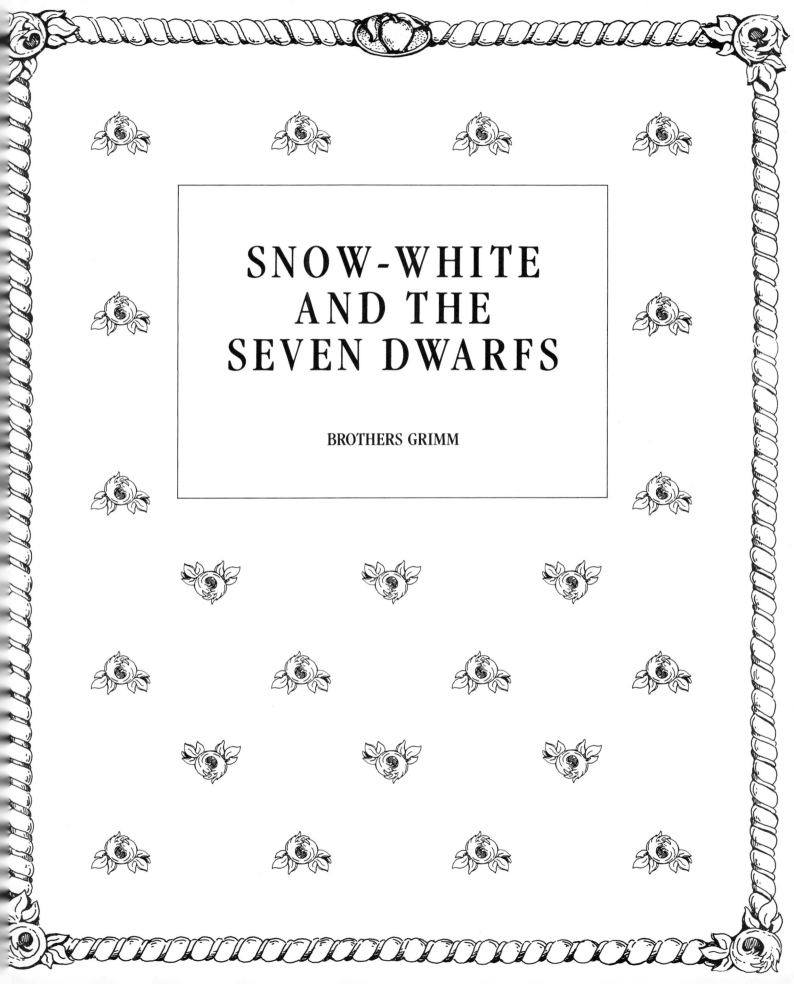

SNOW-WHITE AND THE SEVEN DWARFS

BROTHERS GRIMM

She will see her self.

When the Queen looks in her magic mirror, she sees _____

_____

Once it was the middle of winter, and the snowflakes fell from the sky like feathers. At a window with a frame of ebony a queen sat and sewed. And as she sewed and looked out at the snow, she pricked her finger with the needle, and three drops of blood fell in the snow. And in the white snow the red looked so beautiful that she thought to herself: "If only I had a child as white as snow, as red as blood, and as black as the wood in the window frame!" And after a while she had a little daughter as white as snow, as red as blood, and with hair as black as ebony, and because of that she was called Snow-White. And when the child was born, the queen died.

After a year the king took himself
another wife. She was a beautiful
woman, but she was proud and haughty
and could not bear that anyone should be
more beautiful than she. She had a
wonderful mirror, and when she stood in
front of it and looked in it and said:

**"Mirror, mirror on the wall,
Who is fairest of us all?"**

then the mirror would answer:

"Queen, thou art the fairest of us all!"

Then she was satisfied, because she knew
that the mirror spoke the truth.

But Snow-White kept growing, and kept growing more beautiful, and when she was seven years old, she was as beautiful as the bright day, and more beautiful than the Queen herself. Once when she asked her mirror:

"Mirror, mirror on the wall,
Who is fairest of us all?"

it answered:

"Queen, thou art the fairest in this hall,
But Snow-White's fairer than us all."

Then the Queen was horrified, and grew yellow and green with envy. From that hour on, whenever she saw Snow-White the heart in her body would turn over, she hated the girl so. And envy and pride, like weeds, kept growing higher and higher in her heart, so that day and night she had no peace. Then she called a huntsman and said: "Take the child out into the forest, I don't want to lay eyes on her again. You kill her, and bring me her lung and liver as a token."

The hunter obeyed, and took her out, and when he had drawn his hunting knife and was about to pierce Snow-White's innocent heart, she began to weep and said: "Oh, dear huntsman, spare my life! I'll run off into the wild forest and never come home again." And because she was so beautiful, the huntsman pitied her and said: "Run away then, you poor child."

"Soon the wild beasts will have eaten you," he thought, and yet it was as if a stone had been lifted from his heart not to have to kill her. And as a young boar just then came running by, he killed it, cut out its lung and liver, and brought them to the Queen as a token. The cook had to cook them in salt, and the wicked woman ate them up and thought that she had eaten Snow-White's lung and liver.

Now the poor child was all, all alone in the great forest, and so terrified that she stared at all the leaves on the trees and didn't know what to do. She began to run, and ran over the sharp stones and through the thorns, and the wild beasts sprang past her, but they did her no harm.

She ran on till her feet wouldn't go any
farther, and when it was almost evening
she saw a little house and went inside
to rest. Inside the house everything was
small, but cleaner and neater than
words will say. In the middle there stood
a little table with a white tablecloth,
and on it were seven little plates, each
plate with its own spoon, and besides that,
seven little knives and forks and seven

little mugs. Against the wall were
seven little beds, all in a row, spread
with snow-white sheets. Because she was
so hungry and thirsty, Snow-White
ate a little of the vegetables and bread
from each of the little plates, and
drank a drop of wine from each little
mug, since she didn't want to take
all of anybody's. After that, because she
was so tired, she lay down in a bed,
but not a one would fit; this one was too
long, the other was too short, and so on,
until finally the seventh was just right,
and she lay down in it, said her prayers,
and went to sleep.

As soon as it had got all dark,
the owners of the house came back.
These were seven dwarfs who dug
and delved for ore in the mountains.
They lighted their seven little candles,
and as soon as it got light in their little
house, they saw that someone had
been inside, because everything wasn't
the way they'd left it.

The first said: "Who's been sitting
in my little chair?"

The second said: "Who's been
eating out of my little plate?"

The third said: "Who's been
taking some of my bread?"

The fourth said: "Who's been
eating my vegetables?"

The fifth said: "Who's been using
my little fork?"

The sixth said: "Who's been
cutting with my little knife?"

The seventh said: "Who's been
drinking out of my little mug?"

Then the first looked around
and saw that his bed was a little mussed,
so he said: "Who's been lying on my
little bed?" The others came running
and cried out: "Someone's been lying
in mine too." But the seventh, when he
looked in his bed, saw Snow-White,
who was lying in it fast asleep.

He called the others, who came
running up and shouted in astonishment,
holding up their little candles so
that the light shone on Snow-White.
"Oh my goodness gracious! Oh my
goodness gracious!" cried they,
"how beautiful the child is!" And they
were so happy that they didn't wake her,
but let her go on sleeping in the
little bed. The seventh dwarf, though,
slept with the others, an hour with each,
till the night was over.

When it was morning Snow-White awoke, and when she saw the seven dwarfs she was frightened. They were friendly, though, and asked: "What's your name?"

"I'm named Snow-White," she answered.

"How did you get to our house?" went on the dwarfs. Then she told them that her stepmother had tried to have her killed, but that the huntsman had spared her life, and that she'd run the whole day and at last had found their house.

The dwarfs said: "If you'll look after our house for us, cook, make the beds, wash, sew, and knit, and if you'll keep everything clean and neat, then you can stay with us, and you shall lack for nothing."

Why are the dwarfs so happy to find the beautiful Snow-White?

The Seven Dwarfs Find Snow-White

"Yes," said Snow-White, "with all my heart," and stayed with them. She kept their house in order: in the morning the dwarfs went to the mountains and looked for gold and ores, in the evening they came back, and then their food had to be ready for them. In the daytime the little girl was alone, so the good dwarfs warned her and said: "Watch out for your stepmother. Soon she'll know you're here; be sure not to let anybody inside."

But the Queen, since she thought
she had eaten Snow-White's lung and liver,
was sure that she was the fairest of all.
But one day she stood before her mirror
and said:

"Mirror, mirror on the wall,
Who is fairest of us all?"

Then the mirror answered:

"Queen, thou art the fairest that I see,
But over the hills, where the seven
dwarfs dwell,
Snow-White is still alive and well,
And there is none so fair as she."

This horrified her, because she
knew that the mirror never told a lie;
and she saw that the hunter had
betrayed her, and that Snow-White
was still alive. And she thought and

thought about how to kill her, for as long
as she wasn't the fairest in all the land,
her envy gave her no rest. And when
at last she thought of something,
she painted her face and dressed herself
like an old peddler woman, and nobody
could have recognized her. In this
disguise she went over the seven
mountains to the seven dwarfs' house,
knocked at the door, and called:
"Lovely things for sale! Lovely things
for sale!"

Snow-White looked out of the
window and called: "Good day, dear lady,
what have you to sell?"

"Good things, lovely things,"
she answered, "bodice laces of all colors,"
and she pulled out one that was woven
of many-colored silk.

"It will be all right to let in the
good old woman," thought Snow-White,
unbolted the door, and bought
herself some pretty laces.

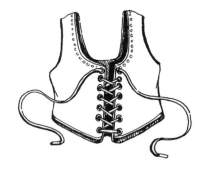

"Child," said the old woman,
"how it does become you! Come, I'll lace
you up properly." Snow-White hadn't
the least suspicion, and let the old
woman lace her up with the new laces.
But she laced so tight and laced so
fast that it took Snow-White's breath away,
and she fell down as if she were dead.
"Now you're the most beautiful again,"
said the Queen to herself, and
hurried away.

Not long after, at evening, the seven dwarfs came home, but how shocked they were to see their dear Snow-White lying on the ground; and she didn't move and she didn't stir, as if she were dead. They lifted her up, and when they saw how tightly she was laced, they cut the laces in two; then she began to breathe a little, and little by little returned to consciousness. When the dwarfs heard what had happened, they said: "The old peddler woman was no one else but that wicked Queen; be careful, don't ever let another soul inside when we're not with you."

But the wicked Queen, as soon as she'd got home, stood in front of the mirror and asked:

"Mirror, mirror on the wall,
Who is fairest of us all?"

It answered the same as ever:

"Queen, thou art the fairest that I see,
  But over the hills, where the seven
    dwarfs dwell,
  Snow-White is still alive and well,
  And there is none so fair as she."

When she heard this all the blood rushed to her heart, she was so horrified, for she saw plainly that Snow-White was alive again. "But now," said she, "I'll think of something that really will put an end to you," and with the help of witchcraft, which she understood, she made a poisoned comb. Then she dressed herself up and took the shape of another old woman. So she went over the seven mountains to the seven dwarfs' house, knocked on the door, and called: "Lovely things for sale! Lovely things for sale!"

Snow-White looked out and said:
"You may as well go on, I'm not allowed
to let anybody in."

"But surely you're allowed to look,"
said the old woman, and she took out the
poisoned comb and held it up. It looked
so nice to the child that she let herself be
fooled, and opened the door. When they'd
agreed on the price the old woman said:
"Now, for once, I'll comb your hair
properly." Poor Snow-White didn't suspect
anything, and let the old woman do as
she pleased. But hardly had she put the
comb in Snow-White's hair than the poison
in it began to work, and the girl fell
down unconscious. "You paragon of
beauty," cried the wicked woman,
"now you're done for," and went away.

By good luck, though, it was almost
evening, when the seven dwarfs came
home. When they saw Snow-White
lying on the ground as if she were dead,

right away they suspected the stepmother
and looked and found the poisoned comb.
Hardly had they drawn it out than
Snow-White returned to consciousness,
and told them what had happened.
Then they warned her all over again to
stay in the house and open the door
to no one.

At home the Queen stood in front
of the mirror and said:

> **"Mirror, mirror on the wall,**
> **Who is fairest of us all?"**

It answered the same as ever:

> "Queen, thou art the fairest that I see,
>   But over the hills, where the seven
>   dwarfs dwell,
>   Snow-White is still alive and well,
>   And there is none so fair as she."

On these two pages, underline some things that you think show how tricky and evil the Queen is.

When she heard the mirror say that, she shook with rage. "Snow-White shall die," cried she, "even if it costs me my own life!" Then she went to a very secret, lonely room that no one ever came to, and there she made a poisoned apple. On the outside it was beautiful, white with red cheeks, so that anyone who saw it wanted it; but whoever ate even the least bite of it would die. When the apple was ready she painted her face and disguised herself as a farmer's wife, and then went over the seven mountains to the seven dwarfs' house. She knocked, and Snow-White put her head out of the window and said: "I'm not allowed to let anybody in, the seven dwarfs told me not to."

"That's all right with me," answered the farmer's wife. "I'll get rid of my apples without any trouble. Here, I'll give you one."

"No," said Snow-White, "I'm afraid
to take it."

"Are you afraid of poison?"
said the old woman. "Look, I'll cut the
apple in two halves; you eat the red cheek
and I'll eat the white." But the apple
was so cunningly made that only the red
part was poisoned. Snow-White longed
for the lovely apple, and when she saw
that the old woman was eating it,
she couldn't resist it any longer,
put out her hand, and took the
poisoned half. But hardly had she a
bite of it in her mouth than she fell down
on the ground dead. Then the Queen
gave her a dreadful look, laughed aloud,
and cried: "White as snow, red as
blood, black as ebony! This time the
dwarfs can't wake you!"

And when, at home, she asked the mirror:

> "**Mirror, mirror on the wall,**
> **Who is fairest of us all?**"

at last it answered:

> "**Queen, thou art the fairest of us all.**"

Then her envious heart had rest, as far as an envious heart can have rest.

When they came home at evening, the dwarfs found Snow-White lying on the ground. No breath came from her mouth, and she was dead. They lifted her up, looked to see if they could find anything poisonous, unlaced her, combed her hair, washed her with water and wine, but nothing helped; the dear child was dead and stayed dead. They laid her on a bier, and all seven of them sat down and wept for her, and wept for three whole days.

Then they were going to bury her, but she
still looked as fresh as though she were
alive, and still had her beautiful red cheeks.
They said: "We can't bury her in the
black ground," and had made for her a
coffin all of glass, into which one could
see from every side, laid her in it, and
wrote her name on it in golden letters,
and that she was a king's daughter.
Then they set the coffin out on the
mountainside, and one of them always
stayed by it and guarded it. And the
animals, too, came and wept over
Snow-White—first an owl, then a raven,
and last of all a dove.

Now Snow-White lay in the
coffin for a long, long time, and her
body didn't decay. She looked as
if she were sleeping, for she was still
as white as snow, as red as blood,
and her hair was as black as ebony.
But a king's son happened to come into
the forest and went to the dwarfs' house
to spend the night. He saw the coffin
on the mountain, and the beautiful
Snow-White inside, and read what was
written on it in golden letters. Then he
said to the dwarfs: "Let me have the coffin.
I'll give you anything that you want
for it."

But the dwarfs answered:
"We wouldn't give it up for all the gold
in the world."

Then he said: "Give it to me then, for I can't live without seeing Snow-White. I'll honor and prize her as my own beloved." When he spoke so, the good dwarfs took pity on him and gave him the coffin.

Why do the dwarfs think Snow-White will be better off with the prince?

Now the king's son had his
servants carry it away on their shoulders.
They happened to stumble over a bush,
and with the shock the poisoned
piece of apple that Snow-White had
bitten off came out of her throat.
And in a little while she opened her eyes,
lifted the lid of the coffin, sat up, and was
alive again. "Oh, heavens, where am I?"
cried she.

The king's son, full of joy, said:
"You're with me," and told her what had
happened, and said: "I love you more than
anything in all the world. Come with me
to my father's palace; you shall be my wife."
And Snow-White loved him and went
with him, and her wedding was celebrated
with great pomp and splendor.

But Snow-White's wicked stepmother
was invited to the feast. When she had put
on her beautiful clothes, she stepped
in front of the mirror and said:

> **"Mirror, mirror on the wall,**
> **Who is fairest of us all?"**

The mirror answered:

> "Queen, thou art the fairest in this hall,
> But the young queen's fairer than us all."

Then the wicked woman cursed and was
so terrified and miserable, so completely
miserable, that she didn't know what to do.
At first she didn't want to go to the
wedding at all, but it gave her no peace,
she had to go and see the young queen.
And as she went in she recognized
Snow-White and, what with rage and
terror, she stood there and couldn't move.
But they had already put iron slippers
over a fire of coals, and they brought them
in with tongs and set them before her.
Then she had to put on the red-hot
slippers and dance till she dropped
down dead.

Why does Snow-White let herself be fooled by the wicked Queen?

_____

_____

_____

_____

Snow-White's Dreams

I remember _____

_____

I feel _____

I remember _____

_____

I feel _____

I remember _____

_____

I feel _____

I hope _____

I hope _____

My Question

_____

_____

_____

Name _____

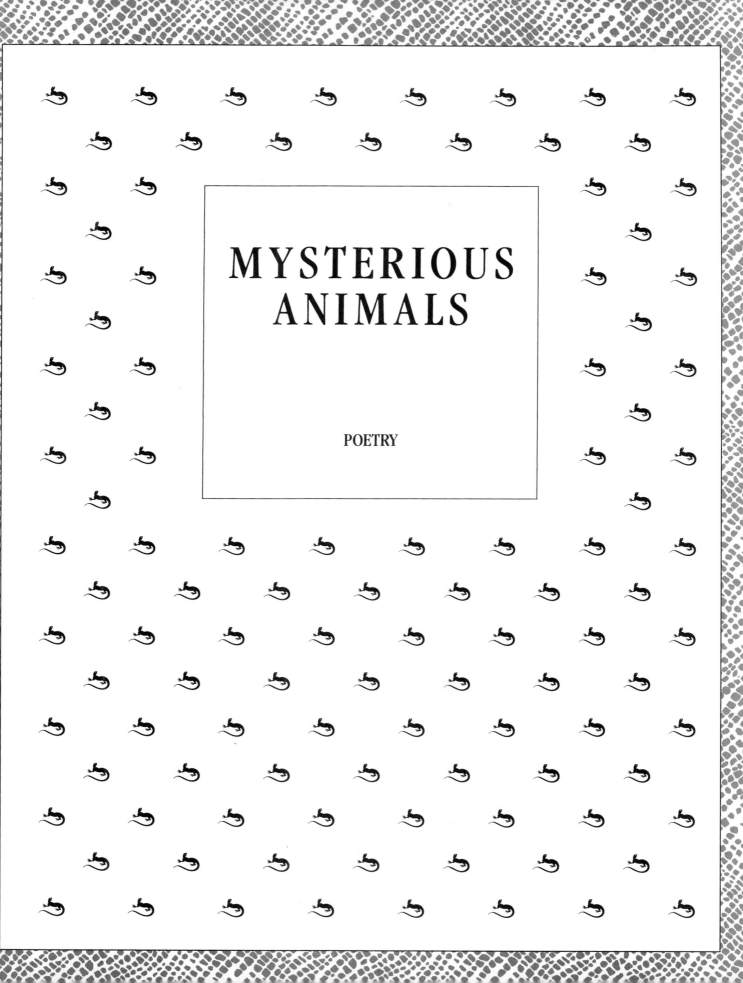

MYSTERIOUS ANIMALS

POETRY

The Jellicle Cats _____

THE SONG
OF
THE JELLICLES

Why would it be fun to be a Jellicle Cat? (Underline some things in the poem that help you answer this question.)

Jellicle Cats come out to-night
Jellicle Cats come one come all:
The Jellicle Moon is shining bright—
Jellicles come to the Jellicle Ball.

Jellicle Cats are black and white,
Jellicle Cats are rather small;
Jellicle Cats are merry and bright,
And pleasant to hear when they caterwaul.
Jellicle Cats have cheerful faces,
Jellicle Cats have bright black eyes;
They like to practise their airs and graces
And wait for the Jellicle Moon to rise.

Jellicle Cats develop slowly,

Jellicle Cats are not too big;

Jellicle Cats are roly-poly,

They know how to dance a gavotte and a jig.

Until the Jellicle Moon appears

They make their toilette and take their repose:

Jellicles wash behind their ears,

Jellicles dry between their toes.

Jellicle Cats are white and black,
Jellicle Cats are of moderate size;
Jellicles jump like a jumping-jack,
Jellicle Cats have moonlit eyes.
They're quiet enough in the morning hours,
They're quiet enough in the afternoon.
Reserving their terpsichorean powers
To dance by the light of the Jellicle Moon.

Jellicle Cats are black and white,

Jellicle Cats (as I said) are small;

If it happens to be a stormy night

They will practise a caper or two in the hall.

If it happens the sun is shining bright

You would say they had nothing to do at all:

They are resting and saving themselves to be right

For the Jellicle Moon and the Jellicle Ball.

—T. S. Eliot

Why do the Jellicle Cats only dance when there is a Jellicle Moon?

My Question

_____

_____

_____

Name _____

IF YOU GO SOFTLY

If you go softly out to the gum trees
At night, after the darkness falls,
If you go softly and call—
    Tch, Tch, Tch,
    Tch, Tch, Tch,
    They'll come—
    the possums!

If you take bread that you've saved
They'll come close up, and stand
And eat right from your hand—
    Softly,
    Snatching,
    Nervous—
    the possums!

And if you are still, and move slowly,
You can, very softly, pat
Their thick fur, gently, like that—

      It's true!

      You can!

      Really touch them—

      the possums!

You can do that all—
If you go softly,
At night,
To the gum trees,
If you go softly
—and call.

—Jenifer Kelly

66

I would like to see a _____

THE SIX BADGERS

As I was a-hoeing, a-hoeing my lands,
Six badgers walked up, with white wands in their hands.
They formed a ring round me and bowing, they said:
"Hurry home, Farmer George, for the table is spread!
There's pie in the oven, there's beef on the plate:
Hurry home, Farmer George, if you would not be late!"

So homeward went I, but could not understand
Why six fine dog-badgers with white wands in hand
Should seek me out hoeing, and bow in a ring,
And all to inform me so common a thing!

— Robert Graves

The badgers are _____

My Favorite Words

_____

_____

_____

_____

_____

_____

_____

_____

_____

Acknowledgments

—

All possible care has been taken to trace ownership and secure permission for each selection in this series. The Great Books Foundation wishes to thank the following authors, publishers, and representatives for permission to reprint the copyrighted material in this volume:

The King of the Frogs, from TALES TOLD NEAR A CROCODILE, by Humphrey Harman. Copyright 1962 by Humphrey Harman. Reprinted by permission of Century Hutchinson Publishing Group Limited.

Snow-White and the Seven Dwarfs, from THE GOLDEN BIRD AND OTHER TALES FROM THE BROTHERS GRIMM, translated by Randall Jarrell. Copyright 1963 by Macmillan Publishing Company. Reprinted by permission of Macmillan Publishing Company.

"The Song of the Jellicles," from OLD POSSUM'S BOOK OF PRACTICAL CATS, by T. S. Eliot. Copyright 1939 by T. S. Eliot; renewed 1967 by Esme Valerie Eliot. Reprinted by permission of Harcourt Brace Jovanovich, Inc.

"If You Go Softly," by Jenifer Kelly, from SOMEONE IS FLYING BALLOONS, compiled by Jill Heylen and Celia Jarrett. Reprinted by permission of the author.

"The Six Badgers," from THE PENNY FIDDLE, by Robert Graves. Reprinted by permission of A. P. Watt Limited, on behalf of the Trustees of the Robert Graves Literary Trust.

Illustration Credits

—

Patti Green prepared the illustrations for *The King of the Frogs.*

Kaye Pomeranc White prepared the illustrations for *Snow-White and the Seven Dwarfs.*

Kate Brennan Hall prepared the illustrations for *"The Song of the Jellicles."*

Emily Arnold McCully prepared the illustrations for *"If You Go Softly."*

"G.B." was created by Ed Young. Copyright 1990 by Ed Young.

Cover art by David Frampton.

Cover and book design by William Seabright and Paul Uhl, Design Associates.